Sheila Lane and M......

KV-197-837

The Knock on the Door
A Play for Christmas

CAMBRIDGE UNIVERSITY PRESS
Cambridge
London   New York   New Rochelle
Melbourne   Sydney

The Knock on the Door
A Play for Christmas

In this book, information from the Bible about the birth of Jesus
has been filled out with stories telling what could have been
happening in the background, at the time of the Nativity.

The first play has a domestic setting in the house of Elizabeth,
and is about the birth of John. The second play, which takes place
in a shepherds' shelter, has a background of family rivalry and
sheep stealing. In the third play there is friction between local
craftsmen, soldiers and dignitaries in a hostelry in Jerusalem, until
the arrival of Astrologers from the East. All meet together in the
fourth play in an inn in Bethlehem, where they pay homage to the
new King.

The stories are linked by songs and carols which can be sung by
a choir or spoken by narrators.

Contents

Every star shall sing a carol   *page*   6

IN THE HOUSE OF ELIZABETH   7

    Carols   22

IN A SHEPHERDS' SHELTER   23

    Carols   37

OUTSIDE A HOSTELRY IN JERUSALEM   38

    Carols   52

AN INN IN BETHLEHEM   53

    Notes   60

    Music for the carols   61

Every star shall sing a carol

(*To be said or sung as an introduction.*)
Every star shall sing a carol;
Every creature, high or low,
Come and praise the King of Heaven
By whatever name you know.
    God above, man below,
    Holy is the name I know.

Every star and every planet,
Every creature high and low,
Come and praise the King of Heaven
By whatever name you know.
    God above, man below,
    Holy is the name I know.

In the House of Elizabeth

Playmakers

ZACHARIAS
ELIZABETH] parents of the baby John

SAUL
SARAH] parents of ten children

NATHAN
NAOMI] a young, childless married couple

ELI   a neighbour
RUTH   his wife
SIMON   their son

GIDEON
MICAH] Temple priests
AARON

ROMAN CAPTAIN
FIRST SOLDIER
SECOND SOLDIER
Other people of the town

In the House of Elizabeth

SARAH *and* NAOMI *come in.* ELIZABETH *follows, carrying a basket of bread.*

ELIZABETH	Now your family will be content, cousin! (*handing bread to Sarah*)
SARAH	My thanks for this bread, Elizabeth. (*sighing*) Sometimes I lie in bed at night and wonder how I shall feed them all. (*raising hands*) So many mouths to feed!
ELIZABETH	But I envy you your large family, Sarah. Children are such a blessing!
SARAH	Are they, Elizabeth? (*laughing*) Then I am blessed ten times over!
NAOMI	Nathan and I pray each day that we shall have a child soon.
ELIZABETH	(*wistfully*) Once I did that, but now I fear it is too late for Zacharias and me. (*cheerfully*) But take heart, dear Naomi! Your time will come.
SARAH	(*to Naomi*) Help me with the basket. Farewell Elizabeth!
	(SARAH *and* NAOMI *pick up the basket of bread and go out.*)
ELIZABETH	(*calling after them*) There will be more bread for you tomorrow, Sarah! (*sighing*) I wish that I had ten mouths to feed.
	(*A loud knocking startles her.*)
	That doesn't sound like Zacharias!
	(*Loud knocking is repeated as she goes to the door.*)
	Have patience! I am coming!
	(ELIZABETH *opens the door and* THREE PRIESTS *come in, followed by a small crowd.*)

GIDEON	Elizabeth, wife of Zacharias our Temple priest, prepare yourself!
ELIZABETH	(*hand on breast*) What is it? Is it my husband? What has happened to Zacharias? Is he . . . dead?
MICAH	No, woman! Zacharias lives.
AARON	He is on his way here from the Temple.
ELIZABETH	Then what is it?
GIDEON	Something has happened . . . but it is a mystery!
CROWD	(*murmur*) A mystery. (*They spread out their hands.*)
ELIZABETH	(*impatiently*) I have no time for mysteries.
MICAH	Elizabeth! There has been . . . in the Temple . . . this very day . . . a most mysterious happening.
CROWD	(*murmur*) A most mysterious happening.
AARON	Your husband, Zacharias, was in the Temple . . . as is the custom . . .
GIDEON	. . . offering up the incense . . . as is the custom . . .
CROWD	(*murmur*) As is the custom . . .
MICAH	. . . and for a long time he did not come out from the sanctuary.
ELIZABETH	(*raising hands*) How slow these men are to tell a tale!
AARON	Zacharias will tell you no tale, woman. (*slowly*) HE . . . IS . . . DUMB!
CROWD	(*wail*) Dumb! Dumb!
ELIZABETH	Zacharias, my husband, DUMB! That I'll believe when I hear it from his own lips.
GIDEON	Woman! Can't you understand? Your husband can no longer speak!
THREE PRIESTS	Zacharias is DUMB!

(ZACHARIAS *walks slowly in and* CROWD *moves back. He points to his mouth and shakes his head.*)

ELIZABETH Husband! Say my name to me! Say,
E-LIZ-A-BETH.

(ZACHARIAS *slowly mouths each syllable and then points to heaven.*)

MICAH That is the sign he gave when he came out from the sanctuary.

AARON It must be that he saw a vision.

CROWD (*nod and murmur*) A vision!

ELIZABETH (*to priests and crowd*) Something has happened which I do not understand. Please leave us, all of you. Go! Go!

(PRIESTS *and* CROWD *go out.*)

Husband! Look on me!

(ZACHARIAS *puts his hands on Elizabeth's head in blessing.*)

My husband blesses me! What can this mean?

(ZACHARIAS *mimes holding and rocking a baby in his arms.*)

A baby! Whose child will this be?

(ZACHARIAS *points to Elizabeth and himself, and smiles.*)

(*not believing*) How can this be? You know I am too old. How . . . ?

(ZACHARIAS *quickly puts his hand over Elizabeth's mouth and then points to heaven.*)

(*shaking head*) This is something . . . which . . . I don't understand. But . . . could it be that one day . . . ?

(ZACHARIAS *and* ELIZABETH *go out, each with hands together in prayer.*)

To indicate passage of time a prayer is sung by the choir or spoken by narrators.

> Abba Father, let me be
> Yours and yours alone.
> May my will forever be
> Evermore your own.
>
> Never let my heart grow cold,
> Never let me go,
> Abba Father, let me be
> Yours and yours alone.

(ZACHARIAS *comes in, moves to bench and picks up a writing tablet.* ELIZABETH *picks up a broom and sweeps the room.*)

ELIZABETH   Zacharias! (ZACHARIAS *looks up.*) I wonder if you really know how I have longed for a child all these years.

(ZACHARIAS *writes.*)

Zacharias! (ZACHARIAS *looks up.*) I wonder if you knew how I felt . . . seeing other women with their families?

(ZACHARIAS *writes.*)

(*sighing*) He doesn't even listen to me!

(*A loud knock on the door.*)

Who knocks so late?

(ZACHARIAS *moves towards the door.*)

Zacharias! We don't want strangers at this time.

(ZACHARIAS *opens the door.*)

Mary!

MARY   (*from doorway*) Elizabeth! Let me in, cousin.

ELIZABETH	Mary of Nazareth! Dearest of all my family! Why have you come so far . . . and at such a late hour?
	(ELIZABETH *puts her hands out in welcome and then quickly holds herself.* ZACHARIAS *and* MARY *hurry to her side.*)
MARY	Fear not, Elizabeth! It is the child you are to have. The child stirs within you.
ELIZABETH	(*in wonder*) Praise be! (*to Mary*) My child is stirring! (*smiling*) The babe jumps for joy!
	(ELIZABETH *and* ZACHARIAS *bow their heads, then quickly look at Mary in astonishment.*)
ELIZABETH	Mary! How could *you* know of this?
MARY	The angel told me.
	(ZACHARIAS *lifts his hands in prayer.*)
ELIZABETH	Angel! Do you mean that . . . you have had a vision? Zacharias! Did you hear? An angel has told Mary of our child who is to come.
MARY	The angel told me of *your* child, Elizabeth, and of another! (*smiling*)
ELIZABETH	Another! Another child? Mary! Do you mean . . . that . . . you . . . YOU . . . ?
MARY	(*bowing her head*) Yes. I am to have a child too.
	(ELIZABETH *and* ZACHARIAS *look at each other in bewilderment.*)
ELIZABETH	How can this be?
MARY	(*stretching out her hands to both*) The Angel Gabriel came to me with greetings. He said, 'Hail, Mary! The Lord is with you.'
ELIZABETH	(*taking Mary's hands*) Mary! Weren't you afraid?
MARY	At first I was very troubled. But then the angel calmed my fears. Elizabeth! Zacharias! I have been chosen . . . to be the mother of the Messiah.

(*Pause.*)

ELIZABETH   (*quietly*) Blessings upon you, Mary! And upon your child! You are indeed blessed among all women. (*smiling*) And blessed am I that the mother of the Messiah should come here on this day.

MARY   (*kneeling and putting hands together*)
My soul doth magnify the Lord,
For he that is mighty hath done to me great things;
And holy is his name.

(MARY *and* ELIZABETH *go out humming or singing:*
'Lully, lulla, thou little tiny child,
By by, lully, lullay.'
ZACHARIAS *follows.*)

The CHOIR *now say or sing Psalm 23, to indicate passage of time.*

The Lord's my shepherd,
I'll not want,
He makes me down to lie
In pastures green, he leadeth me
The quiet waters by.
My soul he doth restore again,
And me to walk doth make
Within the paths of righteousness,
E'en for his own name's sake.

(ELIZABETH *comes in. She lays her baby in the crib, humming,* 'Lully, lulla . . .' *as she does so. She is soon followed by* SARAH *and* NAOMI, *who are carrying a covered basket.*)

SARAH   (*quietly*) Listen! Our cousin is singing.

NAOMI   How happy she is now that she has the child she longed for.

ELIZABETH	(*looking up*) Welcome cousins! (*showing child*) Look at my son! The Lord has been good to me in my old age.
SARAH	(*laughing*) Don't forget that the child belongs to Zacharias too!
NAOMI	How is he? Is he . . . just the same?
ELIZABETH	(*shrugging*) Just the same – still dumb, my poor old Zacharias. But, I must confess, it's peaceful to have a silent man about the place.
NAOMI, SARAH	(*laughing*) Elizabeth!
ELIZABETH	Silence is sometimes golden. Besides, (*looking at baby*) I have other sounds to listen to now. My son is eight days old.
SARAH	(*happily*) Eight days old! This is a day of celebration for us all.
NAOMI	(*pointing to basket*) We've brought gifts for the child's celebration. Look! (*showing gifts*) Salt! Oil! Bread!
SARAH	Enough for a large gathering.
ELIZABETH	A large gathering here in my house for the babe's celebration! Oh, I am indeed blessed! (*She looks towards the door as footsteps are heard.*) Listen! (*excitedly*) More visitors!
	(NATHAN *and* SAUL *come in, carrying a basket of fruit.*)
NATHAN	(*laughing*) Just husbands! The others are on their way.
SAUL	We rejoice to find you in good spirits, Elizabeth.
NATHAN	(*going to crib*) The boy sleeps peacefully.
SAUL	(*laughing*) That won't last long! I should know with all my brood! In no time at all this babe will be full grown.

14

NATHAN	How proud I shall be when I can hold my first-born son in my arms.
SAUL	I remember the first time I held my David – born to us soon after his grandfather died. Yes, I was proud to have a son to carry on my father's name.
ELIZABETH	There is something I want to . . . (*She is interrupted by sounds outside.*) Oh! We have more visitors.

(ZACHARIAS *comes in and greets everyone with signs. He is followed by the* TEMPLE PRIESTS *and* FRIENDS.)

GIDEON	We have brought the child a gift. (*He hands two small black boxes to Elizabeth.*)
MICAH	In them you will find the child's own texts . . .
AARON	. . . which later he can wear, as his forefathers have before him.
GIDEON	Come! Let us look upon the child.
ELIZABETH	There is something that must be told. (*taking a deep breath*) This child is not to be named after the father of Zacharias.
ALL	(*in amazement*) Not to be named after his grandfather!
ELIZABETH	(*clearly*) His name is JOHN.

(ZACHARIAS *holds out a writing tablet and writes:* 'His name is John'.)

ALL	(*in amazement*) JOHN!
ZACHARIAS	(*lifting up arms*) HIS NAME IS JOHN!
ALL	(*in amazement*) Zacharias SPEAKS!
ZACHARIAS	Now I can speak again. God's promise is fulfilled.
ALL	(*fearfully*) How can this be?
ZACHARIAS	(*holding up baby*) Here is God's chosen prophet.

ELIZABETH	(*taking John*) John! God's prophet!
ZACHARIAS ELIZABETH	Praise be to God!
ALL	Praise be to God!
ZACHARIAS	(*to Temple priests*) Let us return to the Temple and give thanks.

(ZACHARIAS *and* PRIESTS *go out, followed by* FRIENDS.)

SARAH	(*putting arm round Elizabeth*) Cousin! Are you afraid?
ELIZABETH	I have no fear. I have known for some time that this child, our John, was being sent to us for a very special purpose. (*She looks up on hearing sounds outside door.*) We have more visitors!

(ELI *and* RUTH *come in.*)

RUTH	(*anxiously*) We thought to find young Simon here.
ELIZABETH	(*slyly*) Perhaps he's not as full-grown as you both believe! Perhaps he's at play!
ELI	(*angrily*) At play! Our Simon is fourteen years old this month.
RUTH	(*proudly*) Our Simon is to become a rabbi.
SAUL	Young Simon . . . a rabbi!
NATHAN	(*to Eli*) Is that *his* choice? Or is it yours?
SAUL	Why, only yesterday I saw him playing games with the Roman soldiers in the market place.
ELI	(*angrily*) With Romans! I have forbidden it! He shall be punished.
NATHAN	(*to Eli*) Can you imagine young Simon in the Temple reading the Torah?

(SIMON *appears at the door.*)

RUTH	Ah! He comes! Simon, what . . . ?

(SIMON *runs in swinging a Roman bulla on a chain.*)

ELI   Stand there, boy! (*pointing to bulla*) WHAT IS THAT in your hand?

SIMON   (*holding up bulla*) Look! Isn't it beautiful? I've exchanged my phylacteries for this Roman bulla.

(ALL *look anxiously at Eli.*)

ELI   (*angrily*) EXCHANGED . . . for that! (*shaking fists in air*) Give me strength to deal with this boy.

SIMON   But father! The Romans give these bullas to *their* sons. The Romans have these charms . . .

ELI   CHARMS! Boy! You know that your phylacteries are sacred objects . . . (*incredulously*) . . . yet you exchanged them for this wicked . . . evil . . . Roman . . . TOY!

SIMON   (*angrily*) It's not wicked! There's no more evil in this . . . (*swings bulla*) . . . than in some of your old objects.

RUTH   (*desperately*) Simon! Guard your tongue.

SIMON   But it's not wicked, mother! (*to Eli*) Just because you hate the Romans . . . just because the bulla is Roman . . . Well, I like the Romans and one day I shall go to Rome.

ELI   (*raising hand to strike boy*) You shall be punished!

SAUL   (*grabbing Eli's arm*) No! Do not strike your son.

ELI   (*wildly*) Can't you all see that the boy is out of my control? I shall go to the Temple Court and consult with the Elders to see what is to be done with him.

(ELI *storms out.*)

RUTH   (*calling after him*) No, husband! Don't do that! (*to others*) The disgrace! Our own son! Brought before the Temple Court! (*sobbing*) By his own father!

SIMON	(*in alarm*) What will they do? Will they come here for me? (*runs to Elizabeth*) Don't let them take me. Say you won't!
ELIZABETH	(*to others*) We must all think what we can do.
RUTH	The Elders are strict. They may come for him.
SAUL	Then we must think of some way to hide the boy . . . until the anger has died down.
NATHAN	(*to Simon*) You must learn to respect your father's wishes.
SIMON	I will! I will!
SARAH	The boy is already sorry in his heart. That is a beginning. Now . . . what can we do?
NAOMI	Look at the crib! (*pointing*) Simon could hide in there.
ELIZABETH	Beside my babe! I won't have that! Besides, he is too big. (*thoughtfully*) But . . . there could be room beneath . . .

(SARAH *and* NAOMI *arrange a cloth over the crib, so that folds hang down.*)

Take heart, Ruth! The Elders may not come at all. Besides, your Eli might go for advice to Zacharias, in the Temple.

RUTH	(*hopefully*) Zacharias! Ah! He will counsel my Eli. (*turning to Simon*) Zacharias could take away some of your father's wrath.

(*The tramping of feet is heard outside.*)

SIMON	(*in fear*) They've come! (*He runs and hides under the crib covers.*)
ELIZABETH	Those are soldiers' feet.

(*Loud knocking is heard.*)

Saul! See who it is.

(ROMAN CAPTAIN *and* TWO SOLDIERS *come in.*)

SAUL Romans! What do you want with us?

CAPTAIN (*surprised*) So many gathered together! I had thought to find here . . . (*looking at scroll*) . . . Zacharias, a priest and Elizabeth, his wife. (*looking around*) No others.

SAUL (*worried*) It is a family celebration for the birth of this boy child, (*indicating crib*) . . . nothing more!

ALL FAMILY (*rather fearfully*) Nothing more!

CAPTAIN Good people! There is no need to fear Roman soldiers! We came to tell the priest of the new decree. Now we can tell you all.

NATHAN (*suspiciously*) What is this . . . decree?

1ST SOLDIER An order . . . from the Emperor . . . in Rome . . .

2ND SOLDIER . . . which must be obeyed by all people in his Empire.

ALL JUDEANS (*looking at each other*) What can it be?

CAPTAIN (*to soldiers*) Read it.

1ST SOLDIER (*reads*) 'Every man and woman shall register in the city of their birth . . .'

2ND SOLDIER Which means that your names will be put down so that you can be counted.

ALL JUDEANS (*looking at each other*) Counted! Why?

CAPTAIN (*laughing*) So that our Emperor, Caesar Augustus, can collect taxes from you all!

ALL JUDEANS (*looking at each other*) Taxes!

CAPTAIN You understand that well enough!

SAUL Our King is Herod. We pay taxes to him.

CAPTAIN And you will pay them to Caesar Augustus also. You've all heard the decree. (*to soldiers*) We must move on. (*to Judeans*) Farewell!

(CAPTAIN *and* SOLDIERS *go out.*)

NATHAN   This is bad news.

SAUL   How can I pay the Emperor in Rome *and* our own King Herod *and* feed my family?

(ALL *murmur angrily.*)

RUTH   (*pulling Simon from under covers*) You're safe now, boy.

SIMON   (*happily*) It was only the Romans!

NATHAN   (*bitterly*) Your precious Roman friends are to count each one of us, so that they can take away the little that we have. How do you feel now?

(ZACHARIAS *and* ELI *come in.*)

ZACHARIAS   Wife! We have just passed Roman soldiers.

ELI   (*agitated*) They came out from this house. I saw them!

ZACHARIAS   Peace Eli! There may be nothing in it!

SAUL   (*bitterly*) NOTHING! That is the word. Soon . . . (*spreading out hands*) . . . soon, we shall all have nothing!

ELIZABETH   (*to Zacharias*) The Romans came here to tell us about more taxes.

ELI   Taxes! I thought . . . (*pointing to Simon*) . . . I thought . . . they had come to take . . .

SIMON   (*running to Eli*) Father! Father! I too have thought in my own way. (*hanging head*) I'm sorry for the hurt I've given you.

ELI   (*putting out hands*) I'll try to be more patient with you, boy. The good Zacharias has counselled me.

SAUL   We've more to think about now than this boy's foolishness. (*angrily*) We have to journey to the city of our birth and then pay more taxes. Is there no end to it all?

NATHAN	The day, which began so well, has darkened. Come Naomi! We must make plans for our journey. (NATHAN *and* NAOMI *go out.*)
SARAH	So must we all. (SAUL *and* SARAH *go out.*)
ELI	Come, wife! Come, my son! (*to Elizabeth and Zacharias*) Farewell to you both and my thanks for your counsel. (ELI, RUTH *and* SIMON *go out.*)
ZACHARIAS	Peace at last!
ELIZABETH	(*quietly*) Zacharias! Have you thought . . . ?
ZACHARIAS	What is troubling you, wife?
ELIZABETH	It's Mary of Nazareth! What will she do now?
ZACHARIAS	What do you mean? Mary is married to Joseph, so all is well.
ELIZABETH	But Zacharias! Mary is married to Joseph of the house of *David*. All the Davids will have to travel to Bethlehem to register their names.
ZACHARIAS	That is so.
ELIZABETH	But the baby is soon to come. How can Mary travel so far now? What will she do?
ZACHARIAS	She will have to travel to Bethlehem with Joseph. Fear not, Elizabeth. Don't we know that, with faith, all is possible? Come, let us pray for her.

(ZACHARIAS *and* ELIZABETH *kneel in prayer by John's crib, as 'Kum ba yah' is sung or spoken.*)

Someone's praying, Lord, kum ba yah,
Someone's praying, Lord, kum ba yah,
Someone's praying, Lord, kum ba yah,
   O Lord, kum ba yah.

(*During the last line,* ELIZABETH *and* ZACHARIAS *walk out quietly, with hands together.*)

END OF FIRST PLAY

Here we go up to Bethlehem

Here we go up to Bethlehem,
    Bethlehem, Bethlehem,
Here we go up to Bethlehem
On a cold and frosty morning.

We've got to be taxed in Bethlehem,
    Bethlehem, Bethlehem,
We've got to be taxed in Bethlehem
On a cold and frosty morning.

Where shall we stay in Bethlehem,
    Bethlehem, Bethlehem,
Where shall we stay in Bethlehem
On a cold and frosty morning?

Little donkey

Little donkey, little donkey,
On the dusty road,
Got to keep on plodding onwards
With your precious load.
Been a long time, little donkey,
Through the winter's night.
Don't give up now, little donkey,
Bethlehem's in sight.

Ring out those bells tonight,
Bethlehem, Bethlehem,
Follow that star tonight,
Bethlehem, Bethlehem.
Little donkey, little donkey,
Had a heavy day.
Little donkey, carry Mary
Safely on her way.

Little donkey, carry Mary
Safely on her way.

In a Shepherds' Shelter

Playmakers

Shepherds of the family of Hezron

ZADOK
GOZAN] elders
AMAZIAH

MIZRA] boys
EZRA

Shepherds, sons of Cush

SIMEON
PHILIP] elders
CALEB

LABAN] boys
LEVI

Shepherds of the family of Gomer

JOB
JACOB] young men
JETHRO

MAHLI] brothers who are thieves
MUSHI

In a Shepherds' Shelter

MIZRA *and* EZRA *walk wearily into the shelter.*

MIZRA   Why do we have to lead our flocks up to these hills?

EZRA   There's nothing up here but scrub grass for the sheep – and thorns for my feet! (*He sits and pulls out thorns.*)

MIZRA   (*sinking down*) What a life! Walking all day . . . and watching all night.

EZRA   (*blowing on hands*) It blows cold! There could be the first snow of winter tonight.

MIZRA   (*wistfully*) I wish I were in Jerusalem . . .

EZRA   . . . or even little Bethlehem!

MIZRA   Think of the bright lights . . . the singing . . . and the dancing . . .

EZRA   . . . and the food and wine!

MIZRA   I'll not stay a shepherd all my life! When I'm old enough I shall find work in Jerusalem.

(ZADOK, GOZAN *and* AMAZIAH *come in.*)

ZADOK   (*angrily*) So you take your ease while others work! It was not like this in my young days!

GOZAN   (*soothingly*) Times change, Zadok. Times change!

AMAZIAH   (*to Mizra*) Come here, boy! Repeat what you were saying to young Ezra here, when we came in.

MIZRA   (*shrugging*) I said . . . I shall not stay a shepherd when I am old enough to find work in Jerusalem.

ZADOK   Do you mean to go against your father's wishes?

GOZAN   What trade will you follow, Mizra? Every boy must learn a trade.

MIZRA	Shepherding is not the one for me. It's too hard and poor.
AMAZIAH	(*pompously*) We of the family of Hezron believe that all work, however humble, is for God.
MIZRA	Well, I don't want to be a humble . . . shepherd! Do you remember the sons of Cush, who shared this shelter with us last year?
EZRA	I remember *them*! They were so poor.
MIZRA	They had been shepherds all their lives, and they had only two score sheep between them *all*.
EZRA	And such sheep! They were so thin and poor.
MIZRA	Do you remember when they lost a sheep? (*laughs*) They mourned its death as if it were a brother!
ZADOK	(*pointing at boys*) Give me patience with this generation!
GOZAN	The good shepherd will lay down his life for his sheep.
AMAZIAH	So it is written in the Torah!
ZADOK	(*looking out*) More shepherds are coming. They're the ones we were talking about just now.
GOZAN	(*calls*) Greetings from the family of Hezron to the sons of Cush!
	(SIMEON, PHILIP, CALEB, LABAN *and* LEVI *come in.*)
	Come and find a place! The boys will make a fire.
	(BOYS *of both families kindle a fire.*)
SIMEON	It's been a cold coming!
PHILIP	But we've lost none of our flock on the way up – not one!
CALEB	Thanks be!
ZADOK	What of your flock this year, brothers? How many?

SIMEON	We've three score – which is the most we've ever had.
PHILIP	Some are weak and poor, but if we can get them through this winter time, we shall be blessed!
	(ALL SHEPHERDS *sit round fire*.)
SIMEON	(*to Zadok*) What of your flocks, brothers?
ZADOK	All in good heart – some twenty score of fat-tailed ewes.
GOZAN	With the new lambs to come, we shall do well this year.
AMAZIAH	It's a good life for simple men of faith.
SIMEON	(*cautiously*) Brothers of the family of Hezron! There is something . . . which we of Cush must ask of you.
CUSH SHEPHERDS	Aye!
ZADOK	Speak! We Hezrons are listening.
SIMEON	It is . . . that we should take a share of the grazing on the south-facing hills . . .
PHILIP	. . . where our ewes will get some good shelter from the weather.
CALEB	(*pleadingly*) Just a share!
CUSH SHEPHERDS	(*anxiously*) Aye! Just a share!
ZADOK	(*aggressively*) What! You sons of Cush on the south-facing hills! We Hezrons take the south – as we have always done. It is our right!
HEZRON SHEPHERDS	Our right!
GOZAN	Besides, our flocks are large. We cannot split them up – some north, some south.
AMAZIAH	We cannot change our practices!
SIMEON	(*despairingly*) Brothers! It's not so much to ask! We've only three score sheep in all.

26

PHILIP	But they're not fat-tailed ewes like yours. Some are thin and weak. We could lose them when the snows come.
CALEB	(*pleadingly*) So give us some *small* share of the south-facing hills, brothers.
ZADOK	No! We cannot change our practices! You must stay in the north, where you belong!
LABAN	(*to Levi*) We only asked for a small share.
LEVI	(*spitting at Mizra*) You Hezrons are not fair!
MIZRA	(*spitting*) Keep your place . . . CUSH!
EZRA	(*aggressively*) I'll take on any son of Cush!

(SHEPHERD BOYS *begin to scuffle, as* JOB, JETHRO *and* JACOB, *come in.*)

JOB	(*mockingly*) See how the good shepherds of the hills quarrel amongst themselves, brothers!
HEZRON SHEPHERDS	(*moving together*) GOMERS!
ZADOK	Why have you come here?
JETHRO	Why not? This is a common shelter for all shepherds.
JACOB	And, we could be of help.
GOZAN	Help! You! That I can't believe!
AMAZIAH	You Gomers are only quick to help yourselves!

(JETHRO *and* JACOB *move menacingly towards* AMAZIAH, *but are pulled back by* JOB.)

JOB	Leave him! These holy Hezrons always set themselves up above the rest of us. (*to Zadok*) Look at this! (*He takes sheep's ear from under tunic.*)
ZADOK	A sheep's ear! Let me see! (*He takes the ear and then examines his hand.*) Fresh blood!

(HEZRONS *crowd round.*)

27

JOB	Could it be one of your fine animals, Hezrons?
ZADOK	No! It's not one of ours. This is not our ear-mark.

(SONS OF CUSH *move forward*.)

SIMEON	(*anxiously examining ear*) Nor is it ours!
PHILIP	Here are the tooth marks of the wolf that did it.
CALEB	But it's not one of ours.
ZADOK	(*to all Hezrons*) Come! We must check our flocks and make sure that all are marked.

(ALL HEZRONS *go out, looking back suspiciously at Gomers*.)

JOB	(*to Cush shepherds*) What is your quarrel with the Hezrons, brothers?
SIMEON	We have no quarrel, Gomers. But our flock is small and poor . . . just three score ewes.
PHILIP	So we asked the Hezrons for a share of the grazing on the south-facing hills.
CALEB	Just a small share, you understand!
JOB	(*scornfully*) A small share! (*to Gomers*) Listen to them! (*to Cush shepherds*) Brothers! You are too meek and mild.
JETHRO	You're like your own sheep . . .
JACOB	. . . waiting for a leader to show the way!
JOB	You should not *ask*! You should demand your rights!
CUSH SHEPHERDS	(*surprised*) Our rights!
SIMEON	The Hezrons are a powerful family. They have always taken what they want.
PHILIP	(*shrugging*) And we sons of Cush have taken what is left.
CALEB	That is the way it's always been.

JOB	Then you sons of Cush will *always* have a small flock.
JETHRO	The weak go to the wall in this world, brothers!
JACOB	You should draw lots for the south-facing hills, as others do.
CUSH SHEPHERDS	(*in astonishment*) Draw lots!
SIMEON	(*to Cush shepherds*) We could ask the Hezrons . . .
ALL GOMERS	No! Demand!
PHILIP	(*shaking head*) The Hezrons will not agree to . . .
ALL GOMERS	Demand!
JOB	Listen, brothers! If they will not agree, you can take your case to the Shepherds' Court in Bethlehem.
CALEB	Bethlehem! (*shaking head*) Bethlehem is a night's walk from here.
ALL GOMERS	Brothers! Demand your rights!
	(HEZRONS *return and listen in astonishment.*)
ZADOK	What is this talk of rights, brothers?
	(GOMERS *push Simeon forward.*)
SIMEON	(*taking a deep breath*) This talk . . . of rights . . . is for our right . . . to a fair share of grazing on the south-facing hills.
ZADOK	(*angrily*) I've told you – the Hezrons have always taken it.
PHILIP	And we poor sons of Cush have always taken what is left.
CALEB	(*taking a deep breath*) So . . . let us draw lots.
ALL HEZRONS	(*disbelievingly*) Draw lots!
SIMEON	You *must* agree, brothers, or we shall go to the Shepherds' Court in Bethlehem. (*firmly*) Our minds are quite made up!

29

(CUSH SHEPHERDS *move together and nod.*)

GOZAN   Peace brothers! There is no need to go to the Shepherds' Court.

AMAZIAH   We can settle this amongst ourselves . . .

JOB   (*taking straws from tunic pocket*) . . . with these straws!

JETHRO   (*holding up long straw*) This long one for the south.

JACOB   (*holding up short straw*) And this one for the north.

ZADOK   (*putting up hand*) Wait! We Hezrons have some twenty score of sheep. You sons of Cush have only three.

GOZAN   That's nearly seven times as many, brothers.

AMAZIAH   If we did agree to draw lots . . . we would need to do it in another way.

ZADOK   (*cunningly*) We won't draw lots, brothers, because your share of the south grazing is just *one* day and night in every seven. One seventh part!

(CUSH SHEPHERDS *whisper together and nod.*)

SIMEON   Perhaps we'll be content with one seventh part. But we'll go first . . . tonight!

CUSH SHEPHERDS   Aye! Tonight!

(HEZRON SHEPHERDS *whisper to each other and nod.*)

ZADOK   (*reluctantly*) So be it!

CUSH SHEPHERDS   Thanks be! (*They go out happily.*)

JOB   Thanks be to us Gomers!

ZADOK   (*pointing to Gomers*) This is your doing! (*to Hezrons*) Tonight we'll stay close by and rest our flocks here in the fold. (*to Gomers*) Do you hear that? We'll be *close by*. There'll be no pickings for your sort!

(HEZRON SHEPHERDS *go out.*)

JOB   (*holding out hands and calling after them*) Our hands are clean, Hezrons! (*showing ear*) They were put off their guard when they saw this ear without a mark upon it. (*looking round*) What keeps Mahli and his brother?

JETHRO   They should have done their work by now.

JACOB   (*pointing*) Listen! They're coming.

(MAHLI *and* MUSHI, *the two sheep stealers, come in.*)

MAHLI   We saw the Hezrons leave the shelter and hid till it was safe.

JOB   How many of their fat-tails did you take?

MUSHI   Two!

JETHRO   Not more?

MAHLI   Two at one time . . .

MUSHI   . . . and safely.

JACOB   (*nodding*) That's what we all agreed. You have done well!

MAHLI   Both have fine fleeces . . . fit for Herod's Court!

MUSHI   The meat will be fat and tender.

JOB   (*rubbing hands*) We should get good prices in Jerusalem. (*looking round*) Now we must get away while it's still safe . . . and before the Hezrons count their flock!

MAHLI   (*moving to side*) Listen! Someone is coming.

MUSHI   Mahli! Away!

(MAHLI *and* MUSHI *run out.*)

JETHRO   (*laughing*) Those two move more quickly than a serpent strikes!

JACOB   Their lives depend upon it, brothers!

(ZADOK, GOZAN *and* AMAZIAH *hurry in.*)

ZADOK (*in surprise*) So you're still here, Gomers!

JOB (*innocently*) You left us to guard the fire, so here we sit and warm ourselves.

GOZAN (*agitated*) Two of our flock . . . two of our finest fat-tailed ewes are missing!

JETHRO (*questioningly*) A wolf . . . a jackal . . . or a bear perhaps?

JACOB What are the signs?

AMAZIAH There are no signs. There had been no struggle.

ZADOK (*very suspiciously*) Two of our ewes, which I knew well by name, have gone – disappeared into the air if that were possible.

GOZAN So! Those sheep stealers came on two legs, not four!

ALL GOMERS (*laughing*) You can't know that!

AMAZIAH Hezrons have been shepherds in these hills for generations.

(MIZRA *runs in.*)

MIZRA Masters! Come! The sheep stealers are out there!

(HEZRONS *run out.*)

JOB (*jumping up*) This could be bad for us!

JETHRO They've had time to get away.

JACOB No!

JOB Listen! (*sounds of angry voices are heard outside*) There's trouble . . .

(HEZRONS *come in dragging* MAHLI *and* MUSHI.)

ZADOK (*to Hezrons*) Tie their thieving hands!

MAHLI Mercy brothers! We're poor men . . .

MUSHI	. . . and have families to feed.
GOZAN	(*to Gomers*) What do you know of these thieves?
ALL GOMERS	Nothing!
AMAZIAH	(*to Gomers*) By the law of Moses – tell us the truth.
MAHLI	They do not know us!
MUSHI	(*to Mahli*) Tell them! I'll not stand alone in this.
MAHLI	(*whispers to Mushi*) Hold your peace, you fool!
	(HEZRONS *move round Gomers.*)
ZADOK	(*to Mushi*) I heard you! (*to Gomers*) You're in this too, as I suspected.
	(HEZRONS *move in, threatening the Gomers.*)
GOZAN	(*holding up hand*) Wait brothers! Listen!
	(*Faint knocking is heard.*)
	Who's there?
	(*Louder knocking as* HEZRONS *move back.*)
AMAZIAH	That was a shepherd's knock upon the rocks.
MIZRA	I heard it too.
	(*Very loud knocking is heard.*)
EZRA	And I! (*running to doorway*)
	(SIMEON, PHILIP *and* CALEB *enter in great haste.*)
SIMEON	(*panting*) Brothers! Brothers!
PHILIP	(*pointing*) Out there! Out there!
CALEB	Out there . . . upon the hillside.
ZADOK	(*picking up staff*) What's the matter?
GOZAN	Sheep stealers?
AMAZIAH	Or – wolves?
SIMEON	(*shaking head*) No! (*looking round*) Brothers! You *must* believe our story.

ZADOK	(*shrugging*) Tell us, brothers, and we will judge for ourselves.
PHILIP	Out there, on the south-facing hills, we saw it with our own eyes.
GOZAN	*Tell* us then, brothers. Tell us what you saw!
CALEB	(*putting arm over eyes*) There was this great light. It blinded me.
AMAZIAH	Light! What was it?
MIZRA	Was it the light from the moon?
EZRA	Or from a great star?
SIMEON	It was the light of the angel of the Lord.
ALL	(*looking at each other in amazement*) Angel? (*murmuring*) How can this be?
ZADOK	(*shaking head*) You're tired from your journey, brothers. You *think* you've seen some sort of vision.
SIMEON	(*firmly*) We all saw . . . and heard. (CUSH SHEPHERDS *nod.*) The angel spoke with us . . . spoke . . . (*smiling*) and then we all heard the NEWS.
PHILIP	At first we were afraid and could hardly listen.
CALEB	(*putting arm over eyes*) I didn't see or hear very much. I was too afraid.
SIMEON	But then the angel calmed our fears and said, 'Behold, I bring you tidings of great joy, which shall be to all people.' (CUSH SHEPHERDS *nod.*) That was how it was said.
ZADOK	But why was it said to *you*? Why should *you* be chosen for this message . . . if it is for *all* people?
SIMEON	What does that matter? (*looking round at the others*) Brothers! What matters is that the Messiah we have all longed for has come amongst us.

34

ALL	(*looking at each other in amazement*) The Messiah! (*murmuring*) Among us!
ZADOK	How was this said? Tell us the words.
SIMEON	(*raising eyes*) 'For unto you is born this day in the city of David, a Saviour which is Christ the Lord.'

(CUSH SHEPHERDS *nod*.)

GOZAN	(*wonderingly*) In the city of David! Why! That is our Bethlehem!
AMAZIAH	(*wonderingly*) So close. (*to Simeon*) Did they say where we should look in Bethlehem?
SIMEON	Yes, yes! The angel said, 'This shall be a sign unto you; ye shall find the babe wrapped in swaddling clothes, lying in a manger.'

(CUSH SHEPHERDS *nod*.)

ZADOK	(*doubtingly*) In a manger? How can this be? A new *king* . . . a Messiah . . . would be born in . . . a great palace . . . in Jerusalem.
PHILIP	(*firmly*) The angel said . . . in Bethlehem . . . in a manger.
CALEB	This is what was said . . . and this we do believe.
SIMEON	And now we shall go straight there! (*moving towards doorway*)
PHILIP	Simeon! What of the boys? They can't be left behind.
CALEB	Laban and Levi must come too. This is for *all* of us.
SIMEON	So be it! We will take our flock. (*smiling*) It is not large!

(CUSH SHEPHERDS *go out*. HEZRON SHEPHERDS *look at Zadok*.)

ALL HEZRONS	What of us?

ZADOK	(*thoughtfully*) We must go too. We too will lead our flocks to Bethlehem.
ALL GOMERS	(*moving forward*) We must *all* go. (*pointing to Mahli and Mushi*) *All of us.*
MAHLI	This news is for all peoples, masters!
MUSHI	So we too must see the King.
ZADOK	So be it! (*to Hezrons*) Loose their bonds! (*looking round*) We will all go to Bethlehem and see this child who has been born.

(ALL *go out as 'Go tell it on the mountain' is sung or spoken.*)

END OF SECOND PLAY

Go, tell it on the mountain

Go, tell it on the mountain,
Over the hills and everywhere,
Go, tell it on the mountain
That Jesus Christ is born.

While shepherds kept their watching
Over wandering flocks by night,
Behold from out of heaven
There shone a holy light.
Go, tell it on the mountain . . .

And lo, when they had seen it,
They all bowed down and prayed,
They travelled on together
To where the babe was laid.
Go, tell it on the mountain . . .

The Virgin Mary had a baby boy

The Virgin Mary had a baby boy,
The Virgin Mary had a baby boy,
The Virgin Mary had a baby boy
And they say that his name was Jesus.
He come from the glory –
He come from the glorious kingdom;
He come from the glory –
He come from the glorious kingdom;
Oh, yes! believer.
Oh, yes! believer.
He come from the glory –
He come from the glorious kingdom.

The angels sang when the baby was born,
The angels sang when the baby was born,
The angels sang when the baby was born,
And proclaimed him the Saviour Jesus.
He come from the glory . . .

Outside a Hostelry in Jerusalem

Playmakers

ACHIM ⎤
SALMA ⎥ silversmiths
RAM ⎦

SAUL ⎤
DANIEL ⎥ tanners
ELAM ⎥
BENJAMIN ⎦

INNKEEPER
1ST ROMAN SOLDIER
2ND ROMAN SOLDIER
Other soldiers

HABAKKUK ⎤ two high-ranking Judeans
JEHOSHOPHAT ⎦

MELCHIOR ⎤
GASPAR ⎥ astrologers from the East
BALTHASAR ⎦

CHIEF PRIEST   spokesman for Herod

Outside a Hostelry in Jerusalem

ACHIM, SALMA *and* RAM *come into the empty courtyard of the hostelry carrying their silver ornaments.*

ACHIM	(*in surprise*) Look! The courtyard's empty!
SALMA	(*holding up ornaments*) And we had hoped to find customers for our silver in this inn.
RAM	(*calls*) Ho there! Innkeeper!
ACHIM	(*disappointed*) We could do better business in the market.
SALMA	Aye! Let's go there!
RAM	Wait! This inn serves the best wine in all Jerusalem. I'll call again. (*calls loudly*) Ho there! Innkeeper! Customers!
VOICE OF INNKEEPER	Coming! Coming! (*He hurries in carrying wine and drinking bowls.*)
ACHIM	What kept you, man?
INNKEEPER	(*serving wine*) I went to see what was going on in the street outside, masters. There was such excitement!
SALMA	Excitement outside, you say! Well, there's none in here and you nearly lost three customers.
INNKEEPER	(*gloomily*) All my customers ran outside when they heard the rumour.
RAM	Rumour! We've heard nothing. What was it?
INNKEEPER	It was put about that King Herod was to ride forth from the palace gates . . .
ACHIM	(*scornfully*) Who would want to see *him*?
INNKEEPER	But masters! The rumour was that he would shower silver coins upon the multitude.
SALMA	(*bitterly*) That will be the day – when Herod gives away his riches!

RAM	We all shower our wealth on *him* – in taxes!
INNKEEPER	(*holding out hand*) Shower some of yours on me, masters, for my good wine.
ACHIM	Last time we came it was five lepta for each measure.
SALMA	(*taking out money bag*) Five lepta it is!
INNKEEPER	No, masters! Six!
SILVERSMITHS	(*in horror*) Six!
RAM	Six lepta for one measure – that's robbery! Last time the price was five. I remember!
INNKEEPER	Prices rise, masters! It happens all the time. Prices go up and up and up! It's only one little lepton more. Besides, you silversmiths are rich and I'm only a poor innkeeper!
ACHIM	(*crossly*) You should have told us before we drank.
SALMA	(*handing over money*) Make sure that next time you don't ask for *seven*!
	(*Four tanners,* SAUL, DANIEL, ELAM *and* BENJAMIN, *come in carrying leather goods.*)
RAM	(*warningly*) Prices rise daily in this tavern, friends! Be warned! (*pointing to Innkeeper*) He's asking *six* lepta for one measure. (SILVERSMITHS *move to one side holding noses.*) Oh, these tanners always stink of leather.
SAUL	*Six* lepta! We can't pay that price! (*to Achim and Ram*) Let's go!
INNKEEPER	My wine is old and sweet – the best in all Jerusalem.
DANIEL	Yes, and we're poor tanners from the valley, come to Jerusalem to trade. But we've sold nothing all day.
ACHIM	Ah! But you've been collecting the King's silver in the streets. What did you get?

40

ELAM	(*gloomily*) Nothing! King Herod did not come!
SALMA	(*scornfully*) Did you think he would? Herod will not give away what he has taken from us.
BENJAMIN	If we're to drink in here, first we must sell. (*showing bags and shoes to silversmiths*) Look at our work, brothers! See! Finest goat skin . . . camel hide . . .

(*A group of noisy* ROMAN SOLDIERS *comes in.*)

RAM	You have customers now, Innkeeper. These Romans have money and to spare!
1ST SOLDIER	(*to Innkeeper*) Bring us your best wine – and plenty of it!
2ND SOLDIER	(*cheerfully*) Ah! This is the life for me! (*calls*) Make your wine sweet and strong, Innkeeper!
ACHIM	(*warningly*) You would be wise to settle the price *before* you drink, Romans.
SALMA	Before today, the price of one measure in this tavern was *five* lepta . . .
RAM	. . . Now it's *six*! Tomorrow it may be *seven* . . . *eight*! Who knows!
1ST SOLDIER	One lepton, more or less – what does it matter?
2ND SOLDIER	(*throwing Roman coin to Innkeeper*) Here! Take this . . . for us all!
INNKEEPER	My thanks, good masters! (*looking at coin*) But . . . but . . . I've never seen a coin like this before! (*to Romans*) Have you no lepta?
1ST SOLDIER	We Romans are not paid in little lepta, fellow!
2ND SOLDIER	Take our good, Roman money! That coin is worth a day's pay. It's gold!
INNKEEPER	I'd rather have lepta all the same. (*to silversmiths*) Look at this! (*showing coin*)

ACHIM   (*puzzled*) This coin is new.

SALMA   (*in consternation*) It's got someone's head marked on it.

1ST SOLDIER   That's the head of Caesar Augustus, Emperor of Rome.

2ND SOLDIER   A better man than Herod, any day! And remember! *Our* Emperor rules here, my friend, and Herod rules *under* him.

INNKEEPER   (*to silversmiths*) Must I take it? What shall I do?

ACHIM   (*weighing coin in hand*) It's heavy and may be worth much.

1ST SOLDIER   The coin is new from Rome – an aureus!

2ND SOLDIER   (*to Innkeeper*) Don't you want it, fellow?

RAM   (*thoughtfully*) It could be worth ten times the value of the wine these Romans drink. (*to Innkeeper*) But you must decide.

INNKEEPER   Ten times the value of the wine! (*stuffing coin in money bag*) I'll keep it! A man must live in these hard times.

(HABAKKUK *and* JEHOSHOPHAT, *two officials from the Court of King Herod, come in swinging fragrance burners.*)

HABAKKUK   This is the place! The best wine in all Jerusalem is served in this inn.

JEHOSHOPHAT   (*looking round in distaste*) And all the rabble come here! Romans too! The place is full of common soldiers!

HABAKKUK   (*to Innkeeper*) We come from Herod's Court! Find us a place apart from all these commoners.

INNKEEPER   (*humbly*) Welcome to my poor inn. (*throwing robe over seat at side*) Over here, fine sirs!

SAUL   (*hisses to Innkeeper*) Now's your chance, Innkeeper! Put your prices up!

(INNKEEPER *goes out.*)

DANIEL   Let's watch and see if he charges six . . . seven . . . eight lepta for a measure!

ELAM   (*bitterly*) It won't matter to Herod's men! (*to other tanners*) It's all money from our pockets that keeps the King's Court in luxury.

(INNKEEPER *returns, serves officials, then goes out.*)

BENJAMIN   All the same, I would not choose to serve King Herod.

SAUL   (*to other tanners*) I've had a thought, brothers! Herod's men are rich. Perhaps we could do business with them?

DANIEL   (*doubtfully*) Perhaps. (*to Elam*) Elam! You try them!

ELAM   (*walking over to officials*) Masters! We have fine goods made from leather.

BENJAMIN   (*showing leather goods*) Will you buy from us?

HABAKKUK   (*putting hand over nose*) How the rabble smell!

JEHOSHOPHAT   Stay where you are! (*swings fragrance burner*)

SAUL   It's our trade, masters!

DANIEL   We're tanners from the valley outside the city.

ELAM   We live there amid the stink of hides and don't notice it ourselves.

BENJAMIN   (*holding up leather goods*) Hmm! Feel these soft hides . . . goat skins . . . the fleece of sheep . . . camel hides . . .

HABAKKUK   (*taking a goat's skin*) This is indeed well done . . . and soft.

JEHOSHOPHAT	(*scornfully*) Rid yourself of these beggars, Habakkuk! (*tosses coins towards tanners*) Here! Take these!
	(TANNERS *draw back.*)
SAUL	(*angrily*) We're not beggars.
DANIEL	(*picking up coins and holding them out*) Keep your money, masters. We don't ask for charity.
HABAKKUK	Let me have this skin. I like it well.
ELAM	Then, master, we'll keep what you have paid for it.
BENJAMIN	(*taking coins from Daniel and tossing them in the air*) And buy a measure each of wine.
SAUL	(*calls happily*) Ho there! Innkeeper! Customers without!
	(*Loud knocking is heard outside.*)
	Who's there?
	(INNKEEPER *hurries in excitedly.*)
INNKEEPER	Strangers without!
DANIEL	First serve your customers within!
INNKEEPER	Masters all! Look upon these travellers!
	(THREE ASTROLOGERS *walk slowly in, stand still and look round.*)
ALL	Strangers!
ACHIM	Who can they be?
SALMA	Look at their clothes!
RAM	They are of another race of men.
INNKEEPER	(*nervously*) Do you . . . can you . . . ?
ACHIM	Who are you?
GASPAR	We are astrologers.

SALMA	Astrologers! (*looking round*) Star followers! Where have you come from?
BALTHASAR	We come from eastern lands.
ACHIM	But, *where?* Which lands? What are their names?
MELCHIOR	Just now, we have come from *your* Jericho.
SALMA	Jericho is only two days' camel ride away. *Where* before that?
GASPAR	Damascus!
RAM	And before that?
BALTHASAR	The camel road from the east.
ACHIM	*Where* before that?
MELCHIOR	There was Baghdad . . .
ALL	(*gasping*) Baghdad!
GASPAR	And before that, there were the high mountains of Mongolia.
ALL	(*looking at each other*) Mongolia!
BALTHASAR	(*looking round*) Is this some kind of lodging house?
INNKEEPER	(*bowing low*) Let me be of service to you, Masters.
MELCHIOR	Bring us refreshment . . . here, in your courtyard. There are others of our retinue outside. Give them what they will.
INNKEEPER	(*bowing*) As you command! (*looking worried*) But . . . but . . . Masters . . . can you . . . (*rubbing palm of one hand with finger*) . . . can you . . . pay?
GASPAR	(*taking small stone from bag*) Take this stone.
INNKEEPER	A stone!
BALTHASAR	It is a jewel, my friend.

INNKEEPER	A jewel! (*rubs hands*) What a day it's been! First a new gold coin from the Romans . . . and now this jewel. (*holding jewel up to light*) I'll keep *this*! A man must live in these hard times! (*He goes out.*)
	(*The* JUDAEAN OFFICIALS *rise and approach the astrologers.*)
HABAKKUK	(*bowing*) Strangers from the East! Tell us, if you will, *why* you have come to Jerusalem.
JEHOSHOPHAT	What is the purpose of your pilgrimage?
MELCHIOR	Our quest is simple. We seek our King.
HABAKKUK	A King you say! Have you no eastern King to serve?
GASPAR	The King we seek will be a father for the whole world!
ALL	(*astonished*) A father! A father for the whole world!
JEHOSHOPHAT	A king who is a father! How can this be?
BALTHASAR	Many moons ago, it was written in the stars, that at this time, a new King would be born . . .
ASTROLOGERS	. . . here! in Judaea!
MELCHIOR	We have followed his star from the East and now our quest is nearly over.
GASPAR	We believe that the child is already born . . .
BALTHASAR	. . . and named, King of the Jews!
ALL	(*astonished*) King of the Jews!
HABAKKUK	The King of the Jews lives here, in Jerusalem.
MELCHIOR	No, it is not Herod whom we seek.
GASPAR	We know of Herod.
BALTHASAR	Our treasures are not for him!
ALL	(*looking at each other*) Treasures!

(HABAKKUK *and* JEHOSHOPHAT *move quickly to one side.*)

HABAKKUK (*to Jehoshophat*) Treasures, they say! They do not look rich but . . .

JEHOSHOPHAT Herod must learn of this! Come! (*They both go out.*)

(INNKEEPER *comes in with refreshment for the astrologers.*)

INNKEEPER Masters! Will you eat olives and fresh bread? Will you drink wine? It is the custom here.

MELCHIOR (*sipping*) The wine is sweet and good!

INNKEEPER Masters! The hour is late! Will you rest here for the night?

GASPAR (*shaking head*) No! We take no rest!

INNKEEPER But I saw your camels outside. They are footsore and weary.

BALTHASAR The little rest we take will be under the stars. We must move on.

(ASTROLOGERS *move to the side with refreshment.*)

ACHIM Did you hear? These strangers spoke of treasures.

SALMA Aye! They did!

RAM Jewels could be hidden inside their robes!

ACHIM Innkeeper! Show us the jewel which these strangers gave you in payment for the wine and olives.

INNKEEPER (*showing jewel*) What is it?

SALMA (*handling jewel*) I don't know, but it could be of great value. (*to other silversmiths*) We could do business here ourselves! (*approaching astrologers*) Strangers from the East! Would you care to see our silver ornaments? (*They crowd round the astrologers.*)

RAM	(*holding up ornaments*) Our work is known all over Jerusalem. (*hopefully*) You will want to take souvenirs back to the East?
	(TANNERS *take out their leather work.*)
SAUL	(*to other tanners*) Brothers! Here is *our* chance to do business with these strangers. (*They crowd round the astrologers.*)
ELAM	This is fine work, masters! Goatskins! Camel hide!
BENJAMIN	Will you trade with us, strangers?
	(SILVERSMITHS *and* TANNERS *call out loudly.*)
SILVERSMITHS	Silver! Silver ornaments!
TANNERS	Goatskins! Camel hides!
	(HABAKKUK *and* JEHOSHOPHAT *come in with the* CHIEF PRIEST *and stand watching.*)
HABAKKUK	(*quietly*) This is the place.
JEHOSHOPHAT	(*quietly*) And these are the travellers from the East of whom we spoke.
CHIEF PRIEST	(*loudly*) You did not say that this inn was a market place!
	(ALL CRAFTSMEN *and* INNKEEPER *turn and become fearful.*)
INNKEEPER	The King's Chief Priest! Here in my tavern! (*hurrying forward and bowing*) What is your will?
HABAKKUK	(*pushing innkeeper aside*) Our business is not with you, fellow!
JEHOSHOPHAT	(*to astrologers*) Strangers from the East! Herod the King, sends his Chief Priest to greet you.
CHIEF PRIEST	(*bowing*) In the name of Herod our King, I bid you all welcome to Jerusalem.
	(ASTROLOGERS *move forward and bow.*)

48

ASTROLOGERS	We thank your King.
CHIEF PRIEST	Herod, our King, has heard of your long journey to this land and would speak with you himself.
MELCHIOR	What could King Herod want with us?
CHIEF PRIEST	He would ask you some questions.
GASPAR	Why would he ask questions of travellers like ourselves?
BALTHASAR	Have we offended against one of his laws?
CHIEF PRIEST	Herod, our King, would ask more about the purpose of your pilgrimage.
MELCHIOR	We have already said . . .
CHIEF PRIEST	(*holding up hand*) The King himself bids you come to the palace and have audience with him . . . and bring with you all your books of learning.
BALTHASAR	We are *astrologers*, not scribes!
GASPAR	We have no books! All that we know is written in the stars.
CHIEF PRIEST	(*puzzled*) Written in the stars! How can this be?
MELCHIOR	(*pointing to sky*) It is written up there, in the stars, that a new King is born . . .
GASPAR	. . . and this new King is a child . . . a new-born babe!
CHIEF PRIEST	(*narrowing his eyes*) And *where, exactly where* . . . shall this child be born?
BALTHASAR	In Bethlehem . . . in Judaea . . . so it is written in the stars.
CHIEF PRIEST	Herod the King must hear this from your own lips. (*cunningly*) You will understand that he will want to find the child, so that he too can worship him. (*taking Melchior's arm*) Come! The King waits to speak with you.

(CHIEF PRIEST *escorts* MELCHIOR, *and* HABAKKUK
and JEHOSHOPHAT *escort other* ASTROLOGERS *out*.)

ACHIM You heard the Chief Priest!

SALMA It could go badly for these Eastern strangers once
they're in Herod's clutches.

RAM Herod could see them as a threat to his power.

(ALL *look troubled and shake their heads*.)

ACHIM Others have been taken inside the palace gates . . .

SALMA and never been seen again!

RAM I would not be in their shoes now for all the
treasures of the Orient.

SAUL These strangers from the East are far from their
homes. They have no families *outside* the palace,
so who will ask questions if they are put away –
for ever?

DANIEL (*thoughtfully*) *We* know!

ELAM (*looking at Daniel*) Yes! We know! And in a way,
these strangers are our brothers.

BENJAMIN (*gloomily*) But what can we *do*? We're all in
Herod's power. We can do nothing! (*angrily*)
Nothing!

(ROMAN SOLDIERS *come forward*.)

1ST SOLDIER Listen! I don't think your Herod will harm these
strangers . . . yet!

2ND SOLDIER He's more likely to make use of them.

. ALL How?

1ST SOLDIER It's the way of all those in power to first make use
of smaller men – before they destroy them.

2ND SOLDIER It's my guess that Herod will persuade these
astrologers to find the child first, then go back and
lead him to the place where the young King is.

50

ALL	To Bethlehem!
SAUL	(*thoughtfully*) If you're right, soldier, then these astrologers are safe for the time being . . .
DANIEL	and could soon be on their way to Bethlehem.

(SOLDIERS *nod and go out.*)

ELAM	(*excitedly*) Brothers! We could go too! We could follow the strangers to Bethlehem.
BENJAMIN	And when the babe is found, the new child King, we too can make our homage.

(ALL *look at each other wonderingly and move towards exit.*)

ACHIM	We'll keep watch for the strangers at the palace gate . . .
SALMA	. . . and follow after them.
RAM	We'll all follow the star.

(ALL *go out as 'Standing in the rain' is sung or spoken.*)

END OF THIRD PLAY

Standing in the rain

No use knocking on the window.
There is nothing we can do, sir.
All the beds are booked already,
There is nothing left for you, sir.
Standing in the rain,
Knocking on the window,
Knocking on the window
On a Christmas Day.
There he is again,
Knocking on the window,
Knocking on the window
In the same old way.

No, we haven't got a manger,
No, we haven't got a stable.
'Till you woke us with your knocking,
We were sleeping like the dead, sir.
Standing in the rain . . .

All poor men and humble

All poor men and humble,
All lame men who stumble,
Come, haste ye, nor feel ye afraid;
For Jesus, our treasure,
With love past all measure,
In lowly poor manger was laid.

Though wise men who found him
Laid rich gifts around him,
Yet oxen they gave him their hay:
And Jesus in beauty
Accepted their duty;
Contented in manger he lay.

An Inn in Bethlehem

Playmakers

INNKEEPER
HANNAH   his wife

MARY
JOSEPH

MATHAN
REBEKAH   his wife
Their children

SOLOMON
ESTHER   his wife
URI   their son
Other children

From the second play

SIMEON ⌉
PHILIP |
CALEB | the Cush shepherds
LEVİ |
LABAN ⌋

From the third play

MELCHIOR ⌉
GASPAR | the astrologers
BALTHASAR ⌋
Other followers-on from the first three plays

An Inn in Bethlehem

SOLOMON, ESTHER, URI *and* CHILDREN *arrive in the courtyard of the inn in Bethlehem.*

SOLOMON   (*looking round*) Bethlehem at last! How quiet it is!

ESTHER   Aye husband! Five o'clock in the morning and all Bethlehem is asleep. (*sighs*) I wish that I had a place to lay my head.

URI   We should have rested in the last village, father.

SOLOMON   No! We're late for the registration as it is.

ESTHER   Look at our young ones, husband! They need food.

SOLOMON   (*looking up*) Dawn is breaking! Soon this inn will open up.

URI   Look up there! (*pointing to sky*) Over the inn! That single star shines more brightly than the rest.

SOLOMON   Perhaps it's a good omen for us all.

(MATHAN, REBEKAH *and* FAMILY, *come into the courtyard from another direction.*)

MATHAN   (*to his family*) Look over there! We're not the only ones who have come late to Bethlehem for the counting.

REBEKAH   They will be of the family of David too.

SOLOMON   (*turning round*) Did you say David? We're of that family.

MATHAN   Greetings to all Davids!

(*The* TWO FAMILIES *exchange greetings.*)

SOLOMON   We were talking of that star (*pointing*) when you came. Look! Over the inn! That one has stayed on into the dawn.

(ALL *look up.*)

ESTHER (*impatiently*) Stars! Stars! All this talk of stars! It's food and rest that we need now.

REBEKAH It's time this inn opened up for early morning travellers such as ourselves.

SOLOMON I'll try the door. (*pushes*) It's barred! We shall have to wait.

(HANNAH *hurries across courtyard from side, carrying a large, covered bread basket.*)

HANNAH Aye! That you will! You must all wait. (*stopping*) And let that door be – or you'll get nothing!

MATHAN (*eagerly*) Woman! Is there bread in your basket?

SOLOMON We can pay well for it.

HANNAH I've nothing for any of you.

MATHAN Don't you want trade?

HANNAH I've too much trade already with Bethlehem so full! (*pulls off basket cover*) Look! My basket's empty. I must bake more. Now let me by. (*She hurries out.*)

SOLOMON (*sighing*) What shall we do? Our families must eat. I'll try the door again. (*pushes door*) It's still barred. (*calls*) Ho there! Open up! Open up!

ALL (*call*) Open up! Open up!

URI Listen! I can hear someone coming!

(*The door opens and* INNKEEPER *appears.*)

INNKEEPER (*angrily*) Hold your peace, out there!

MATHAN Peace be to you, Innkeeper!

INNKEEPER (*yawning*) Don't you know the hour?

SOLOMON Innkeeper! We've travelled many miles to Bethlehem for the registration.

INNKEEPER	If it's rooms you want . . . I have none! (*He turns to go.*)
MATHAN	(*holding Innkeeper's arm*) Listen! We've come a long way and must find a place to rest.
REBEKAH	You must have a place somewhere.
INNKEEPER	I've told you – there's nothing here . . . even the stable's full. (*He looks up and sighs.*) More travellers!

(SHEPHERDS *enter in great excitement.*)

SIMEON	Innkeeper! We're shepherds from the hills and have come to Bethlehem to seek . . .
INNKEEPER	(*interrupting*) To seek rooms! As they all do! Well, I haven't any.

(HANNAH *hurries in.*)

PHILIP	No! Not rooms! We've come to Bethlehem to seek . . .
HANNAH	(*interrupting*) To seek bread! As they all do! Well, I haven't any and there'll be none until mid-day. I've other things to do.
CALEB	No! Not bread! We've come to Bethlehem to seek the child . . . who is our new King . . . our Messiah.
SIMEON	We shall find him lying in a manger.
INNKEEPER	What do you mean? (*to Hannah*) How can these shepherds know of the birth?
HANNAH	We've told no one.
INNKEEPER	(*to shepherds*) There *has* been a birth . . . (*pointing*) . . . there, in our stable.
HANNAH	Shepherds! Tell us more.
PHILIP	News was brought to us as we kept watch over our flocks out on the hillside.

INNKEEPER	(*quietly*) What do you mean? How was this news brought . . . and *who* brought it?
ALL SHEPHERDS	The angel of the Lord came to us!
SOLOMON	(*to others*) What do these shepherds mean? (*to shepherd boys*) You boys! Tell us what happened.

(LABAN *and* LEVI *move towards the families.*)

LABAN	There was this great light in the sky . . .
LEVI	. . . and from the light came the angel of the Lord.
MATHAN	Weren't you afraid?
LABAN	No, because the angel told us not to be troubled . . .
LEVI	. . . and then told us about the baby.
ESTHER	What else?
LABAN	The angel said that the baby would be born in Bethlehem . . .
LEVI	. . . and would be our Saviour.
REBEKAH	Was there to be . . . a sign?
LABAN	Ah yes! The angel said, 'This is your sign – you will find the baby . . . wrapped up . . .
LEVI	. . . and lying in a manger.'
HANNAH	(*wonderingly*) When that couple arrived here from Nazareth . . .
INNKEEPER	. . . we had no room for them in the inn.
HANNAH	So we put them in the stable, where the woman could rest because her time had come. Then . . . later . . . the child was born. It was a boy and they laid him in the hay.
SIMEON	(*nodding wisely*) This child will be the one we seek.
PHILIP	He who is to be our King and Saviour – our Messiah!

CALEB	(*to other shepherds*) He for whom we have been searching.
LABAN	(*moving towards stable door*) Is this the stable?
LEVI	(*knocking on stable door*) Is HE in there?
	(BOTH BOYS *bang on door which is opened by* JOSEPH.)
JOSEPH	Who knocks so loudly on the door?
LABAN, LEVI	(*joyfully*) We do!
JOSEPH	Hush! You will wake the child.
LABAN	But we've come to see him.
LEVI	Look! We've brought a lamb.
URI	(*pointing to sky*) The star's still there, over the stable. (*to his family*) That is *our* sign too.

(MARY *enters from stable, with child, while all sing:*

Infant holy,
Infant lowly,
For his bed a cattle stall;
Oxen lowing,
Little knowing
Christ the babe is Lord of all.

(*Loud knocking is heard as verse ends.* LABAN *and* LEVI *run towards side door.*)

LABAN	There are more visitors, Innkeeper.
LEVI	(*happily*) There will be more, and more, and MORE!
URI	The whole world will come!
INNKEEPER	(*hurrying over to side door*) Come in! Come in!
	(ASTROLOGERS *come in.*)
LABAN	(*astonished*) Strangers . . . from another land!

LEVI	Look at their clothes.
URI	Who can they be?
SOLOMON	(*to boys*) Peace! (*to astrologers*) Greetings in God's name!
	(ASTROLOGERS *bow and all acknowledge greeting in their own way.*)
MELCHIOR	(*pointing upward*) The star, which we followed for so long, stays still above this place.
GASPAR	(*holding out hands towards Mary and baby*) Here is the one whom we seek . . . our Saviour King.
BALTHASAR	Unto us a child is born, Unto us a Son is given.
MELCHIOR	And the government shall be upon his shoulder . . .
GASPAR	And his name shall be called Wonderful, Counsellor . . .
BALTHASAR	The Prince of Peace.
ALL	(*indicating child*) The Prince of Peace! (ASTROLOGERS *present gifts.*)
	(*The arena becomes crowded as characters from other plays enter.* ALL *sing verses 1, 3 and 4 of: 'O come, all ye faithful'.*)

1 O come, all ye faithful,
   Joyful and triumphant,
   O come ye, O come ye to Bethlehem.
   Come and behold him,
   Born the King of angels;
       O come, let us adore him,
       O come, let us adore him,
       O come, let us adore him,
           Christ the Lord.

3   Sing choirs of angels,
      Sing in exultation,
      Sing, all ye citizens of heaven above,
      Glory to God
      In the highest;
          O come, let us adore him . . .

4   Yea, Lord we greet thee,
      Born this happy morning,
      Jesus, to thee be glory given;
      Word of the Father
      Now in flesh appearing;
          O come, let us adore him . . .

Notes

bulla	a small, round Roman charm, made of metal
phylacteries	small leather boxes containing verses of scripture, still used by orthodox Jews today
lepton	(plural – lepta) very small bronze coin, about the size of a ½p, used throughout Judea
rabbi	the chief official of a synagogue – a teacher
Temple	a synagogue, the Jewish place of worship and meeting
Torah	the revealed will of God as contained in the first five books of the Old Testament

Music for the carols

Every star shall sing a carol

Further reproduction of this carol is not permitted under any blanket licence system or otherwise. Reprinted with permission from Stainer & Bell Ltd.

Bind us together Bob Gillman

The Lord's my shepherd

Kum ba yah

Here we go up to Bethlehem

Little donkey

Go, tell it on the mountain

The Virgin Mary has a baby boy

Standing in the rain

All poor men and humble

Infant Holy

O come all ye faithful